UNIVERSITY OF MINNESOTA

John Steinbeck

BY JAMES GRAY

UNIVERSITY OF MINNESOTA PRESS • MINNEAPOLIS

Printed in the United States of America at
the North Central Publishing Company, St. Paul

Library of Congress Catalog Card Number: 74-633323
ISBN 0-8166-0597-1

PUBLISHED IN GREAT BRITAIN, INDIA, AND PAKISTAN BY THE OXFORD
UNIVERSITY PRESS, LONDON, BOMBAY, AND KARACHI, AND IN CANADA
BY THE COPP CLARK PUBLISHING CO. LIMITED, TORONTO

JOHN STEINBECK

JAMES GRAY, literary critic, novelist, and historian, is a former professor of English at the University of Minnesota and former literary editor of the *Chicago Daily News* and of the *St. Paul Pioneer Press–Dispatch.* He is the author of another pamphlet in this series, *Edna St. Vincent Millay.*

⤳ *John Steinbeck*

S O M E among the distinguished array of American novelists who volunteered as witnesses to what life was like in the half century after World War I now seem rather far removed from us. The writers who developed themes that were highly personal to their own experience stand apart. Ernest Hemingway, though he exercised enormous influence on the taste, and even the thinking, of the young in his time, has become an aloof presence only the more withdrawn from us because his gifts were so original and striking. His obsession was with crises of courage dramatized, in his best novels, against a background of foreign wars. He seems to be less a product of our tradition than a titan of ego and energy existing in a world all his own. William Faulkner saw his corner of the American world through a Gothic mist of shock and surprise and the high talents used to evoke this strange realm seem to belong to another age and to a place not quite our own.

Other of the novelists of this time have remained close to us because of their preoccupation with the continuing problems of American life, because of their ability to depict a physical, social, and psychological environment that quickens in us a sense of immediacy and recognition. Two such were F. Scott Fitzgerald and John Steinbeck. Between them they divided up the American world of their era. Fitzgerald took as his share the domain inhabited by the rich, the sheltered, the frequenters of cafés, bootleggers' parties, and psychiatrists' consulting rooms. He found pity and terror among these people and had both moving and ominous things to say about his discoveries. Steinbeck, for his inheritance, took the orchards and growing fields of California, the wasteland of the Depression, the refugee camps of rebels and the slums of poverty. He helped himself also to a scientific laboratory and certain places into which men retire to meditate. He, too, found pity and terror among his fellow human beings but, like Fitzgerald, he also found beauty, charm, and wit. Though the two men would never have thought of themselves as collaborators, they shared the responsibility of presenting in fiction all the conflicts that have confused our time and yet confirmed its aspirations.

Steinbeck speaks to us with special immediacy because in a curious way he anticipated attitudes toward the human experience which have particularly engaged the intelligences of the young in recent years. Many of Steinbeck's characters seem to have been the forebears of the rebels who have gathered in centers of protest from Greenwich Village to the Haight-Ashbury district of San Francisco. What can the dissidents of *Tortilla Flat, Cannery Row,* and *Sweet Thursday* be called but dropouts from society who have the same reasons for rejecting old patterns of belief as do members of the hippie generation? On the negative side the credo of today's young revolutionaries seems, like that of Steinbeck, to have been influenced by a pervasive disillusionment with the gospel of success, by contempt for what seems to them to be cynical commercialism, and by resentment of arbitrary authority. On the positive side, as their banners insist, they wish to be guided — again as were the group-conscious residents of Cannery Row — by a preference for love over the destructive impulses of human nature. Steinbeck accepted as early as the 1930's the obligation to take a stand in his writing against tendencies in the American way of life to which the campus rebels of the present have been making vigorous objection.

More than this, however, Steinbeck never forgot the crucial character of the confrontation between man and his destiny. In the least sober of his books, *Sweet Thursday*, he slipped in a statement which succinctly sets forth his own fundamental belief: "Men seem to be born with a debt they can never pay no matter how hard they try. It piles up ahead of them. Man owes something to man. If he ignores the debt it poisons him, and if he tries to make payments the debt only increases, and the quality of his gift is the measure of the man." The novels, plays, and short stories of this conscientious artist represent successive efforts to pay his debt to man. Wide in the range of their interests, diverse in mood, passionately concerned in their sympathies, they all celebrate the worth of man. For that integrity Steinbeck demands justice and respect; to that integrity he lends the support of his own conviction that all men everywhere are and must be inextricably identified with their kind. Much more clearly than in the instance of any other American writer of his time Steinbeck's consistent effort to establish the dignity of human life offers the measure of the man.

He was born (on February 27, 1902) into an environment that served well to develop his inclinations and to satisfy his needs. The Salinas Valley of California provided a physical setting in which majesty and menace were mixed. Its alternate promises of fertility and threats of drought woke wonder in a sensitive, plastic nature and stirred an alert intelligence. He developed a passion for all the sounds, scents, and tastes of things, animate and inanimate. These crowded in upon him making him conscious, as he once expressed it, of "how the afternoon felt." The sentient boy, recognizable in transfiguration as Jody in *The Red Pony*, was father to the sentient man. And it was in his youth that Steinbeck seized on the belief, which remained with him always, that he shared with all living things the same essence and the same destiny, that there is a oneness of man with men and man with nature.

Spontaneously investigative and responsive from the first, the young Steinbeck found himself in a family setting that he could enjoy. Its assets included many books from among which the boy chose what he needed to serve the purposes of his self-education: Malory, Milton, Shakespeare, Dante, Goethe, Dostoevski, and Thucydides. That he digested instruction well is evident in the enduring influence that many of these guides had on his own work. The oneness of human experience was real to Steinbeck in relation to time as well as to space. What he read seemed to be not about events and passions of far away and long ago but rather, as he observed, "about things that happened to me."

His family, neither rich nor poor, made up a comfortable community the members of which helped each other when they could but encouraged any show of initiative and independence. The father, always unobtrusively sympathetic to the younger Steinbeck's desire to become a writer, once paid, out of a small salary as an official of city government, a minute allowance which kept him in the bare necessities of life while he worked at his manuscripts. The mother as a girl had been a schoolteacher and, though she did not want her son to become a writer and would have preferred to see him established in a profession of acknowledged prestige, she set him on the long search for enlightenment through books.

Olive Hamilton Steinbeck appears briefly on the autobiographical periphery of the novel *East of Eden*, a creature of intense feeling, "as intuitive as a cat," but incapable of disciplined thought. Her theology, Steinbeck wrote, "was a curious mixture of Irish fairies and an Old Testament Jehovah." This naive effort to integrate unlike deities in a Pantheon all her own dazzled the imagination of her son and Steinbeck's fiction was to receive great drafts of refreshment from mythology. He did not hesitate to give to a character of his own creation traits which he had first perceived in figures as unlike as Christ, Faust, and the lord of Camelot. From one or another of the great fables, read in his youth, he borrowed here an intimation, there an insight. These stories were for him myths "which have their roots in reality." In his tireless inves-

8

tigation of their roots, he refined and enriched what he had absorbed under his mother's unsophisticated instruction—and placed it in logical perspective. She had tried to obliterate any reality that threatened her whims either by refusing to believe in it or by raging blindly against it. Steinbeck's own reconciliation with reality became in the end complete. "Things are as they are," he wrote, "because they must be."

Though his logic was cool his temper was not. All his work steams with indignation at injustice, with contempt for false piety, with scorn for the cunning and self-righteousness of an economic system that encourages exploitation, greed, and brutality. What saved him from the helpless vexation against frustrating reality that characterized his mother was in part his humor, which exercised a sanative and corrective influence on all his judgments, and in part his belief in oneness, in "a kind of wholeness to sense and emotion": "Good and bad, ugly and cruel all [are] welded into one."

Throughout the five years of Steinbeck's intermittent attendance at Stanford University (where he did not in the end bother to earn a degree) he worked at odd jobs usually involving physical labor — rancher, road worker, hod carrier, deck hand, cotton picker. He found these occupations congenial because they brought him into intimate association with the great company of workers among whom he chose his friends long before he used them as models for characters in stories. These were men whose courage he admired, whose rejection of cant and hypocrisy he applauded, and whose "high survival quotient" became for him the essential proof of a human being's success.

The man was ready for his work at twenty-seven when he published his first novel, *Cup of Gold* (1929). During the next quarter of a century he produced copiously: eleven novels (*To a God Unknown*, 1932; *Tortilla Flat*, 1935; *In Dubious Battle*, 1936; *The Red Pony*, 1937; *The Grapes of Wrath*, 1939; *Of Mice and Men*,

1940; *The Moon Is Down*, 1942; *Cannery Row*, 1945; *The Way-ward Bus*, 1947; *The Pearl*, 1947; *East of Eden*, 1952), as well as two collections of short stories (*The Pastures of Heaven*, 1932; *The Long Valley*, 1938), dramatizations of two of his novels (*Of Mice and Men*, 1940; *The Moon Is Down*, 1942) and a play in story form (*Burning Bright*, 1950), a documentary (*The Forgotten Village*, 1941), two volumes of reportage (*Bombs Away*, 1942, and *A Russian Journal*, 1948), and a journal of travel and scientific research (*Sea of Cortez*, 1951). His performance from the start was accomplished and professional: his books were carefully designed according to artistic principles of his own. The results were often moving, always disturbing, and in several instances strikingly impressive.

There were still two novels to come (*Sweet Thursday*, 1954; *The Winter of Our Discontent*, 1961), and a variety of other publications. But the later phases of Steinbeck's work were largely disappointing to thoughtful critics. That they were disappointing to the writer himself is made clear by a confession which, with a total lack of histrionism, he introduced into *Travels with Charley* (1962). This account of a trip made across the United States with his pet dog is as much an experiment in self-discovery as it is an effort to rediscover America. It contains a scene in which the lonely traveler listens to a fire-and-brimstone sermon preached by an old-fashioned fundamentalist in a Vermont pulpit. Steinbeck reports that he took this indictment of human frailty to himself: "I hadn't been thinking very well of myself for some years." It was at this precise moment that the Nobel Prize for literature was belatedly and almost apologetically awarded him. The vehement protest that the selection roused from many commentators must have made the laurels weigh on his head like a crown of thorns.

Steinbeck did no more significant work. Because he had not lost his taste for the art of communication he took to writing journalistic pieces like *America and Americans* (1966). This study of the native scene is steadily appealing and often shrewdly, though generously, critical. But a tone of autumnal melancholy broods over its pages.

His private life cannot have been without conflict, for he was married three times and divorced twice. However, certain shy liftings of the veil upon his privacy which occur in *Travels with Charley* indicate that his last marriage was happy and that the way of life it brought him — complete with cabin boat on Long Island, town house in New York, and loyal friends — was congenial.

His outlook changed in many ways. A return to Salinas showed him that, as Thomas Wolfe had also found, "you can't go home again." The boys in the back room of his favorite bar were no longer the brothers in spirit that they once had been. And in one significant way Steinbeck was surprisingly out of sympathy with the young whose protests he had so articulately anticipated: he sided with the hawks on the issue of war in Vietnam. Despite these ironies of psychological change, the end of his life did not forget or reject its beginnings. Steinbeck's last intimate communication to his following, contained in a chapter of *Travels with Charley,* expresses, with a ringing echo of the old anger, the "weary nausea" he experienced as he watched a "demoniac" crowd in New Orleans baiting a frightened black child as she entered a previously all white school. In the midst of momentary despair, his pity and pride were invested as deeply as ever in the fate of the miserable and the dispossessed.

John Steinbeck died on December 20, 1968, in New York City.

While he lived Steinbeck was regarded by many of his critics as a kind of perennial apprentice. He experimented with many forms and, as he once boasted a little boyishly, none of his books was like any other. He seemed always to be beginning anew and this suggested to some that he lacked a sense of direction. Doctrinaire critics tended to dismiss any claim that might be made for him as an artist of rank and even the most sympathetic of his contemporary appraisers temporized with a cautious attitude of "waiting to see." Now that the record is complete a dispassionate inspection of his work and an assessment of his accomplishment are in order.

It says something significant about the importance of Steinbeck's work that the testimony must be examined on several different levels of interest. The same can be said of comparatively few American writers up to the very recent phantasmagorical/psychedelic experimentation with forms of fiction. Earlier storytellers conformed to familiar methods, producing, like Edith Wharton, the novel of manners; like Sinclair Lewis, the novel of social satire; or more or less like the master Henry James, the novel of subtle inquiry into states of mind induced by exquisite crises of loyalty. Below such enduring figures as these stood the great mass of fictioneers who ground out replicas of the well-made novel all having similarly stupefying patterns of predictable climaxes.

In contrast, Steinbeck from the moment when he made his debut with *Cup of Gold* was ever an audacious creator of new worlds. Exploring as broadly as possible the secrets of the species man, he presented himself simultaneously as storyteller, fabulist, critic of social institutions, innovative stylist, and appraiser of experience in philosophical terms. In all these roles Steinbeck struggled to give the upper hand to the original over the banal, to fresh intuition over accepted doctrine or dogma, to generous values over shabby ones, and to personal observation over the clichés of image, emotion, or conviction. The degree of success that he attained must be examined separately for each of the roles he played.

That Steinbeck was a storyteller of persuasive power is clear. Always the quintessential dramatist, he demanded of a reader that he identify himself with a particular moment of crisis. Then, by selecting the most revelatory bits of evidence, he wooed his audience subtly but insistently into acceptance of whatever he wished the meaning of an incident, an event, or a passion to be.

The story called "The Chrysanthemums" (from *The Long Valley*) presents the problem of the artist in conflict with philistinism. It does so in a way that makes a familiar, but often drearily detailed, complaint seem immediate and moving because the storyteller has offered a small, unexpected, fully dramatized instance. A woman whose painstaking creativity has been invested in growing flowers is persuaded to give some of her precious sprouts to a man who, while he pretends to warm sympathy with her work, is in fact only exploiting her dedication to gain a petty advantage for himself. When she finds that he has thrown away her sprouts as worthless she suffers the shock of an encounter with insensate brutality. Imbedded in the narrative, which is tense despite its seeming casualness and powerful despite the modesty of its material, is the further implication that to be touched by meanness, even accidentally, is to be a little tainted by it. A struggle to maintain her integrity ends in failure for the once sturdy woman when she finds that vengeful hatred has transformed her into a feebly weeping victim.

André Gide was an admirer of Steinbeck's stories, likening some of them to the best of Chekhov. What these talents have in common is an economy of means which yields a wealth of implication. Steinbeck's attack on what he wished to unmask and to destroy was far more aggressive than that of Chekhov but equally effective. He knew how to touch the sensitive area.

It is one thing to be able to improvise telling incidents and quite another to build a solid narrative out of such materials. In *The Grapes of Wrath* Steinbeck demonstrated that he was indeed master of this technique. His expertness of craftsmanship was not, however, evident to some critics when the novel first appeared. One even said that *The Grapes of Wrath* was as formless as a novel could manage to be. To such critics this seemed to be a haphazardly charted odyssey unworthy of its classical model in that it lacked a hero, like Homer's, whose various adventures were held together by his compelling drive to escape danger and find his way home. Yet this is, in fact, precisely the pattern that *The Grapes of Wrath* does possess. Instead of one central figure there is the family of the Joads, dispossessed tenant farmers of Oklahoma who take to the highway in a collapsing truck. These people are in flight from danger even as Odysseus was; they, too, are trying to find their way home, to a new home which will give them a secure way of life and enable them to achieve dignity. The encounters they have along the way — across the desert, toward the orchards and growing fields of California — are not merely random adventures but the meaningful events of a vigorous struggle for survival.

Viewed from the perspective of the present day, three decades after its first appearance, *The Grapes of Wrath* seems not merely a "proletarian novel," to be dismissed for its vulgar, fleeting timeliness, but an admirably modeled work of art having impressive size and just proportion, movement, balance, symmetry, and power. Each incident representing the struggle of the Joads against time and fate is precipitated onto the stage with the persuasiveness of immediate crisis: the loss of a machine part essential to the operation of the truck; the perilous crossing of the desert in a decrepit vehicle; the betrayal of the workers by landowners who lower wages below subsistence level simply because there is a surplus of fruit pickers; the cynical parody of the rule of law and order in which men wearing badges as deputy sheriffs turn their guns on men who want nothing but the right to support their families; the herding of itinerant workers into squalid camps; the cunning defense by the group of laborers against gross injustice, against the threat of extinction of their kind. Each event in this crucial series is precisely, dramatically defined; each is articulated into the next; the mass of happenings is formed into a climax; the climaxes gain in power until the significance of the group adventure is impressively clear.

The essential point made by this study of the plight of man under the conditions of the Great Depression is that, no matter how bitter the assault on its existence may be, the group will defend itself unyieldingly. It obeys what Steinbeck called in the *Sea of Cortez* "the one commandment for living things: Survive!"

This is what he is able, with the aid of a rich variety of demonstrations, to persuade us is true of the Joads and of the group that forms around them. The families seem to disintegrate; the old members die of hunger and exhaustion; those who expose themselves to special danger as leaders are beaten and one is killed; some of the young people defect through moral weakness or in the service of self-interest. But even as the old group falls apart, a new one is seen to be forming. Tom Joad will become the leader of a new and better trained army fighting for the survival of his kind.

A literary device used by Steinbeck to amplify the meaning of his story may have been what made the book appear formless to certain eyes. Not infrequently he interrupts the flow of narrative to introduce chapters of comment and generalization. One is reminded by them of the way in which the chorus of a Greek play intervenes in the action. These passages contain parables dealing with the problem of survival and with the intricacies of the economic system in which the Joads find themselves inarticulately enmeshed. Abstract though these discussions are, and theoretical, they preserve the tone of drama and parallel the concerns of the story itself.

One of these sections describes, with an air of tension that might be appropriate to the detailing of a performance of a high-wire circus act, the dogged behavior of a turtle crossing a road, evading the purgatorial horrors of highway traffic and finally achieving its goal in the dust of a sheltered place. This minute spectacle dramatized in essence the meaning of the struggle in which the Joads are engaged.

In another of these excursions into allegory Steinbeck dramatized the unending debate between man and a powerful institution which he himself has created but whose vast, impersonal power now threatens to destroy him. The bank which owns the land on which people like the Joads live must put it to more profitable use than tenant farming. The inadequate worker must be put off and his house bulldozed to the ground. "The bank," says the oracle of this ingenious side drama, is "something more than men . . . It's the monster. Men made it, but they can't control it." Thus, without indulging in the moralizing rhetoric of the more usual proletarian novel Steinbeck establishes his point. Man, as victim of his own technological skill, must learn patiently to unweave the noose around his neck.

The Grapes of Wrath does not stand alone as evidence of Steinbeck's storytelling skill. The earlier novel *In Dubious Battle* (still surprisingly neglected) is virtually a model for a certain kind of craftsmanship. Hard, tight-packed as a bullet in its form, its propulsive power matches its theme. *In Dubious Battle* is like *The Grapes of Wrath* in no way except that both books are concerned with workers in a California valley who test fate by defying the power of a growers' association. If *In Dubious Battle* had been intended as a strikers' handbook it could hardly have been more explicit about the tactics of conflict, more scrupulously factual in its concentration on the events of one crisis in full ferment. The novel's unity of time and its strict enclosure within the limits of a particular place give it a classical sharpness of design. Within that pattern the style is as native as the scene is peculiarly American. The language is blunt, colloquial, emphatic, the mood resolute and impersonal.

As the novel opens the wage scale in the apple orchards of Torgas Valley has been dropped in direct proportion to an increase in the number of available pickers. A Communist organizer, Mac, precipitates himself into the situation, assuming a proprietary right to any battlefield of frustration and discontent. Influenced by his delicate manipulation, the workers walk off the job. Mac sees little hope for this particular strike but foments its violence with dedicated zeal and with great skill in the strategy of disruption. In the interest of his party's war on capitalism he maneuvers this skirmish toward its foredoomed tragedy.

When this book was first published Steinbeck was accused of harboring Communist sympathies. Because his strikers are presented as men suffering from unbearable wrongs it was possible for a heedless or prejudiced reader to assume that the novel constituted an endorsement of any movement that promised to correct these wrongs. But the author of *In Dubious Battle* remains as coolly detached as his characters are hotly involved. He puts his own attitude into the mouth of a young doctor who has come voluntarily to this battleground simply to patch up broken heads. Doc is challenged by Mac to clarify his position. "If it rains good and hard tonight the men'll be sneaking out on us. They just won't take it, I tell you. It's a funny thing, Doc. You don't believe in the cause, and you'll probably be the last man to stick. I don't get it at all." And Doc responds: "I don't get myself. . . . I don't believe in the cause, but I believe in men. . . . I have some skill in helping men, and when I see some who need help, I just do it."

Steinbeck's realistic concept of society ("Things are as they are because they must be") had no room in it for any but a clinical interest in a system like that of communism. Its theories seemed to him not merely arbitrary but degrading. One of the most revealing scenes of *In Dubious Battle* exposes a professional revolutionary, the young apprentice, Jim, indulging in an almost orgiastic love of violence for its own sake. Steinbeck's distaste for such doctrinaire dedication is evident. Uncommitted to any cause but the affirmation of the dignity of man, he offered *In Dubious Battle* as a study of the way in which the compulsive behavior of a group may threaten its own survival. It threatens, he seems to insist, and yet cannot finally defeat. Like Doc, Steinbeck did not believe in causes but in men. His novel comments on the problem of man's conflict with his environment, suggesting with a kind of somber optimism that though a battle may end in stalemate the war itself is not lost. The end of *In Dubious Battle* implies a new beginning, satisfying the principle of catharsis.

East of Eden presents Steinbeck in a contrasting facet of his role as storytelling craftsman. The longest of his novels, it manages to be intimate and personal in tone, establishing itself as a kind of genial father-confessor among his books. The contrast with *In Dubious Battle* is complete; one is as diffuse in interest as the other is compact; the later is as full of conversational perambulations as the earlier is severely shorn of such devices. A diary Steinbeck kept for the benefit of his editor during the composition of *East of Eden*, and published posthumously, throws curiously little light on his creative method. But it is clear that in this effort he drew his inspiration from the symphonic form of which he was a devoted student. Into the novel he weaves three themes. Each is given its major and minor variations which play upon each other with harmonic intricacy, producing crescendos of cumulative power. The motifs reveal their interrelationships with ever increasing lucidity so that in the end the work is discovered to be a hymn to earth and to man as protector, expander, and fulfiller of its destiny.

The first motif may be identified by the word "westering." The compulsive movement of men and women across a sea and a continent, to establish a new society in a setting foreign to its origins but sympathetic to its needs, is dramatized in the chronicles of two families, the Hamiltons out of Ireland and the Trasks out of Connecticut. They come together in the Salinas Valley, there to enact the scenes that are vital to Steinbeck's story of a new creation, this time the creation by man of his own world. This is, however, no usual family record of getting and spending, begetting and dying. The events are numerous, spectacular, often violent. They involve all the inevitable crises of conflict ranging from personal feud to war itself. But these concerns of individuals are offered as evidence that a far more significant story is in the process of unfolding. Steinbeck defines westering as the impulse of the group to transform itself into "one great crawling beast" compelled by the secrets of its nature to move through perils, survive disaster, and "get there." This is, in effect, an account in allegorical terms of the great yearning of man ever and again to reenact the drama of Genesis.

The second motif searches out the personal compulsions which in each individual underlie the urgent thrust of the will to survive. In each generation of the family of Adam Trask the conflict of Cain and Abel is paralleled. This, Steinbeck suggests, is "the symbol story of the human soul" and he undertakes to explore the maze of hostilities through which each man must make his way in the inevitable struggle for dominance of brother over brother. The same fateful pattern of ambivalence is evident in the relationship of father and son. As Steinbeck's spokesman observes: "The greatest terror a child can have is that he is not loved, and rejection is the hell he fears. I think everyone in the world to a large or small extent has felt rejection. And with rejection comes anger, and with anger some kind of crime in revenge for the rejection, and with the crime guilt." Steinbeck's two versions of the passion of Everyman, dramatized in Adam Trask's struggle first with a violent brother and then with a difficult, demanding, sensitive son, play contrapuntally on each other until the significance of each phase is fully revealed. The "story of mankind" has been restaged, losing none of its complexity, in the homely setting of the Trask household. The purpose of the author in doing so is, again in the words of his spokesman, to show how many "pains and insanities" could be "rooted out if the causes were known."

The third motif is also a familiar one but it is given a new variation. What Steinbeck contributes to the discussion of humanity's Problem One — the conflict between good and evil — is his own concept of the doctrine of free will. Again he refers to the biblical story recalling that the Lord, in the severity of His love, says to Cain: "If thou doest well, shalt thou not be accepted? and if thou doest not well, sin lieth at the door. And unto thee shall be his desire, and thou shalt rule over him." Steinbeck became convinced that the King James version of the Bible erred in its translation of the significant word in this passage, the Hebrew verb *timshel*. His redefinition makes it a word not of command but of counsel: thou mayest, rather than thou shalt, rule over sin.

When the book first appeared a brisk controversy arose over Steinbeck's interpretation of the meaning of *timshel* and over his spelling of the word as well. Scholars challenged both and then a second group of scholars challenged the first. Steinbeck, beset and defended, held his ground with characteristic self-assurance. In the absence of divine guidance in the matter he may be allowed to accept responsibility for his philosophy and for his orthography as well.

For him the difference between thou shalt and thou mayest works a peaceful revolution in the world of morality. Man ceases to be the slave of unintelligible forces over which he has no control; he becomes master of his destiny when he is given "the glory of the choice" between good and evil. It was Steinbeck's philosophy to the end of his life — as his Nobel address revealed — that three wills are operative in man's experience: the will of the group, the will of the individual, and the moral will which must in the end prevail over the lesser two.

John Steinbeck

East of Eden is parable, poem, and tale of action all in one. Like Melville's *Moby Dick* it finds a meeting ground for physical and spiritual adventure, exploring skillfully the interests of both.

For contrast to this amplitude of design one may turn to an entirely different example of Steinbeck's technical skill. *Of Mice and Men* is so essentially dramatic in its structure that to adapt it to the requirements of the theater it was necessary only to compress its descriptive passages into stage directions and allow the remaining dialogue to take command. Here in the simplest possible terms Steinbeck offers a statement of his belief in the importance of a voluntary acceptance of responsibility. It reminds us again that "man owes something to man."

The central character, George, is a typical Steinbeck figure, a man of the humble workaday world who, as migrant worker, has shown a high survival quotient both in physical resourcefulness and in independence of mind. But his freedom is grotesquely limited by the fact that he has assumed guardianship over a creature of monumental ineptitude, a retarded child in a man's huge body. Lennie's great hands, not being under the control of an adult conscience, cannot resist the temptation to touch and caress any soft thing they encounter. A mouse will do but a girl is better. Inevitably he brings trouble down upon the ill-matched pair wherever they try to settle as workers.

On a ranch where George finds employment for both the fateful routine is enacted again. The provocative, amoral wife of the ranch boss's son attracts Lennie's limited but disastrous interest. What Lennie's weakness urges him to touch his strength compels him to kill. To run away from the fear of punishment is the only wisdom available to the totally inadequate creature and he obeys it. The search that follows must, if it is successful, end in a ritual murder of revenge. George is obliged to find his pitiful friend before the posse can do so and shoot him as an act of kindness.

21

The novel's climactic scene has been anticipated by one having exactly the same import. The stench of an old dog, owned by one inmate of the ranch barracks, has become intolerable to the other men. He is destroyed in all decency — even with respect for his blameless integrity as ranch animal — by one bullet aimed at the back of his head. The point of the parable is explicitly made: no life is unworthy of reverence, not that of an ailing dog, not that of an idiot. Life must be sacred even to a man who is obliged to destroy in order to save.

The small book of related sketches called *The Red Pony* has been overpraised as Steinbeck's best artistic achievement. One may well agree that this portrait of a sensitive boy is indeed distinguished without finding the work as a whole satisfactory. Seldom has the identification of a fledgling artist with the natural scene that surrounds him been presented with a lyricism so innocently appealing. But the structure is topheavy. The one decisive act in this study of an approach to maturity occurs in the first episode, leaving the others to taper off in successive stages of anticlimax. When the boy, Jody, beats in frantic rage at the buzzards hovering over the body of his beloved dead pony, managing to kill one, he declares his sentiments and his loyalties with dramatic eloquence. In the other experiences of the story he is revealed with steadily less ingratiating poignancy. An interesting comment on Steinbeck's preoccupation with problems of technique is to be found in the fact that when he prepared his own scenario for a film version of *The Red Pony* he corrected his mistake by putting the climax where it belongs — at the end.

It is the vocation of the storyteller to communicate to readers a sense of life lived outside the confines of their own skins and beyond the limitations of their own intelligences. To respond to such an evocation is to become momentarily a new man, quickened in flesh, mind, and spirit to new awareness and alerted also to the powerful influence of a certain setting upon all the sensibilities. A world unlike one's own is all at once made intimately familiar.

A writer may be a genius without possessing this special gift of persuasion. Edith Wharton once — quite innocently as she insists in her memoirs — made the confidence of Henry James falter by asking: Why do your characters seem never to have any other place to go when they leave the printed page? James's abashed acknowledgment that he did not realize this was so made tacit confession to certain limitations in his art.

Another highly gifted novelist, John O'Hara, in his stories of conflict over crises in manners, ambitions, and loyalties made do with a similarly restricted realm of creativity. His characters exist tantalizingly, pugnaciously within the space of each well-contrived scene in which they play their parts. But absence from the next scene suggests only that they are being hastily repaired for the ardors of another passage in a love duel or for the rigors of a still more intense struggle for domination in the immediate situation.

The total environment of Steinbeck's world is quite different. Its physical manifestations — the menace of a desert, the peril of flood in a valley — are introduced not as mere stage effects; their impacts fall as awesomely on the reader as they do on the Joad family in *The Grapes of Wrath*. In *East of Eden* the unwritten scenes of Aaron Trask's yearning for identification with his father tug at the imagination with implications of an unappeased desire that grows even during the author's silences. It is the novelist's method to cut into the midst of a scene that seems to have been in progress before the factual report begins and to go on after it closes. The loyalties and hostilities of the hobo jungles that give the setting to *In Dubious Battle* constitute a way of life that seems to draw energy from forces far beyond the arbitrary control of a mere contriver of happenings. The variety, urgency — even the quirkiness — of the mental adventures of many of Steinbeck's characters suggest a richness of experience the like of which is to be found only in the work of the important Russian writers. Indeed it might be said of his novels, as Virginia Woolf said of Dostoevski's, that they are "composed of the stuff of the soul."

Because his creations seem to leap over the barriers of lines on a printed page into an existence of their own, Steinbeck must be credited with distinguished success not merely as storyteller but as reflector of the quality of contemporary American life.

Steinbeck's gift as fabulist contributed heavily to making his work unique among American writers of his time. His borrowings from literature's wealth of folklore and his evident desire to show a kinship between many of his chief characters and the towering figures of myth are evident in *The Grapes of Wrath* and *East of Eden.* But it is in a comparatively obscure early novel, *To a God Unknown,* that his concern with man's heritage from the past is most apparent. This is a book of striking interest, strewn tantalizingly with samples of what he himself described as "the harvest of symbols in our minds [which] seem to have been implanted in the soft, rich soil of our pre-humanity."

The novel may be read on its surface as another story of westering. Joseph Wayne finds the Vermont farm on which he has lived with his father and brothers too small to satisfy his land hunger and, with the blessing of his parent, leaves home. "After a time of wandering," he comes at last to a promising valley of California. He feels close to the land, nourishes its needs, sends for his brothers to join him, becomes the acknowledged patriarch of his clan, marries, loses his wife, faces disaster from drought, and literally gives his life to the soil he loves.

But Steinbeck means to imply much more in this allegory of man's unity with nature. Joseph Wayne is not merely a priest of natural religion; he is one of its demigods, feeling himself to *be* the land, to embody its urgencies, its trials, its failures, and its fulfillment. When at the end he dies by his own hand he regards the sacrifice as having ritualistic significance. Relief from drought immediately follows the use of a knife on the veins of his wrist and he thinks in triumph: "I am the land . . . and I am the rain. The grass will grow out of me in a little while."

Steinbeck did not edge timidly into this large-scale parable of man as "symbol of the earth's soul." He welcomed its challenges boldly. His Joseph Wayne insists upon believing that his dead father has come to live in a tree that stands beside his door; he puts his child into the tree's branches to receive its benediction; he accepts the death of the tree as warning of disaster to come. With these alliances to the occult he passes out of the realm of everyday reality into the realm of mysticism where he reveals his kinship to a cult of primitive deities. A novel must offer many demonstrations of its theme and Steinbeck with his virtuosity of invention finds no difficulty in dazzling a reader with references, back and forth through time, to precedents of wonder. His Joseph is related in the genealogy of letters to Joseph of the Bible who also brought his brothers into a new world, established his authority over the people of a country not his own, and created a society for the protection of all. But Joseph Wayne's ancestry may be traced back farther still to forebears in the primitive world. He is entirely at home among neighbors who engage in rites to propitiate the gods and who, when their incantations seemed to be answered in signs of benediction, erupt lustily into orgies. Even the blood sacrifices of animals in which another neighbor engages, with exquisite skill accompanied by sensations of joy, neither surprise nor appall him.

What must be accepted in order to receive the intended impression of this long prose poem to nature is that Joseph is a creature of earth belonging not to a particular moment in time but, like any figure in mythology, to all time. Or, as the spokesman for Steinbeck's mysticism says: ". . . he is all men. The strength, the resistance, the long and stumbling thinking of all men, and all the joy and suffering, too . . ." There is in him something of the majesty, the harshness, and the detachment of a natural element. What adds greatly to the surprise and high excitement of this conceit is that Steinbeck has been able to give to so extraordinary a being a local habitation and an American name.

A phrase which Steinbeck has used to describe this kind of exercise is "the working of atavistic magic." Surrender of disbelief may not be easy in the face of so unexpected a demand, but the reward of making the effort is a kind of pleasure that is also rare and unexpected. A haunting music flows from every page and the novel's many incantations are alive with what one of the Hindu scriptures calls "right rapture." There is evidence in *To a God Unknown* that, in devising a myth of his own out of a blend of old and new, familiar and remote, Steinbeck was under the influence of Eastern literature. The book's title is derived from a Hindu poem in which these lines occur:

> He is the giver of breath, and strength is his gift.
> The high Gods revere his commandments.
> His shadow is life, his shadow is death;
> Who is He to whom we shall offer our sacrifice?

This impulse to refresh imagination at whatever font world literature may offer was not unlike that of Emerson who, in his hymn to Brahma, celebrated the same esoteric faith that Steinbeck bespeaks in *To a God Unknown*. "Shadow and sunlight are the same . . . one to me are shame and fame."

It is the task of the novelist to capture the universal in the particular, revealing the elusive in intriguing incident. Working in *To a God Unknown* with materials of a peculiarly volatile kind, Steinbeck managed to reduce his favorite theme of unity to the explicit terms of dramatic parable.

26

A better known example of his skill at mythmaking gives a droll turn to the enterprise. *Tortilla Flat* encloses a group of ironic anecdotes within the framework of a romance which claims kinship with the medieval spirit represented by the legend of King Arthur and his Knights of the Round Table. The preface offers this clue to the author's intention: "This story deals with the adventuring of [Danny and] Danny's friends, with the good they did, with their thoughts and their endeavors. . . . It is well that this cycle be put down on paper so that in a future time scholars, hearing the legends, may not say as they say of Arthur and of Roland and of Robin Hood — 'There was no Danny nor any group of Danny's friends . . . Danny is a nature god and his friends primitive symbols of the wind, the sky, the sun.' This history is designed now and ever to keep the sneers from the lips of sour scholars." Obviously Steinbeck's fluent tongue is, for the moment, lodged snugly in his cheek. This is a grandiose joke. Out of his boyhood love of Malory he has fashioned, still in boyish temper, a good-natured parody of the chivalric tradition. Danny, King Arthur's comic counterpart, is a California paisano, recently returned from World War I. He takes into his house a group of strays ardently devoted to indolence who range through the neighborhood of Monterey seeking liquor, women, and whatever fight may help to while away the afternoon. Their "endeavors" are all exuberant parodies of the questing of Arthur's knights.

The loosely linked incidents are mildly bawdy and Steinbeck's treatment of each is ironically indulgent. It is his gleefully maintained pretense that every drunken bout is a grand ceremonial of comradeship and every buffoonish encounter between the sexes a fine display of chivalric spirit. The success of *Tortilla Flat* rests solidly on Steinbeck's complete savoir-faire in maintaining his own air of gravity. A comic miniature of heroic romance, the book keeps its proportions, its emphases, and its implications all in scale, cor-

responding neatly to those of the myth of the Round Table. Even
when Danny dies, in a fall from a cliff after a drunken party, it is
solemnly suggested that he has not been lost to humanity; rather,
he has been "translated" to be forever, again like Arthur, "the once
and future king."

What this parallel treatment of the Arthurian legend implies is
that the first prerequisite for knighthood is generosity. And no matter how grotesque the vagaries of Danny and his friends, they are
in lively possession of qualities that Steinbeck genuinely admires:
virility, honesty, and comradeliness. They are able to make accom-
modation to circumstance and by that adaptability they manage
to survive. Danny's house becomes the symbol of man's environment; the resourceful ways of its inhabitants offer suggestions
which are by no means wholly frivolous about how that environment can be made livable.

Steinbeck's one failure in the realm of mythmaking is the play
in story form called *Burning Bright*. Here he attempted to re-cre-
ate Everyman or, perhaps more nearly, the universal father. The
central situation is that of a man who, though he does not know
of his disability, cannot have a child of his own because he is
sterile. In an effort to restore his self-esteem his wife enters into an
otherwise meaningless relationship with another man so that she
may become a mother. This so closely duplicates a crisis of Eugene
O'Neill's *Strange Interlude* that Steinbeck must have believed it to
be as legitimate to borrow from one's contemporaries as to borrow
from the classics. To the appropriated material he adds something
that is entirely his own: the idea that a mature intelligence must
accept the oneness of humanity. At the close of the play the protagonist, having learned the truth about the child's paternity, is
still able to say: "I love my son." This endorsement carries with it
the implication that in a good society every man should consider
himself to be the father to every son.

The difficulty with the experiment is simply that it does not come off. As in no other of Steinbeck's works the language is uninterruptedly high-flown and artificial. Even the structure seems labored and clumsy: to emphasize the universality of his characters Steinbeck gives them the same names throughout but in each act presents them in a different social setting, first in a circus, then on a farm, and finally against the background of the sea. Even so, Steinbeck's Everyman dwindles into Everystereotype. The interest of *Burning Bright* collapses under the burden of its moral purpose which burns only too ardently.

Entirely successful, within the more modest limits of its intent, is the parable called *The Pearl*. In the *Sea of Cortez* Steinbeck tells of hearing a story about a Mexican Indian pearl diver who found such a fine jewel that he knew "he need never work again." Possession of this rare object so poisoned the existence of the fisherman, however, that he cursed it and threw it back into the sea.

Steinbeck's comment on the story, made in *Sea of Cortez*, was that he did not believe it: "it is far too reasonable to be true." But this uncharacteristic literal-mindedness presently gave way to a realization that the legend cried out for elaboration and interpretation. Showing a fine respect for the special quality of the material, he produced a touching story of good in desperate struggle with evil. An infant becomes his symbol of innocence betrayed. The baby, born to a pearl fisherman, Kino, and his wife, Juana, is bitten by a scorpion and the local doctor refuses treatment because he knows the family to be poor. The situation is reversed when it becomes known that Kino has found "the Pearl of the World." Everyone becomes eager to exploit his ignorance. The doctor tries to play on a father's fears for the child, hoping to get the pearl in payment for useless services. The dealer in pearls belittles the jewel thinking to get it for little. Thieves set upon Kino in the dark trying to rob him and beat him viciously in the attempt. His house is burned in

the course of another invasion. Crises mount until Kino realizes
that he must try to escape from a world that has turned into an
implacable enemy. But there is no escape from the evil that has
been loosed into this community. Kino is tracked into the moun-
tains where he has taken wife and child to hide. Bullets from the
gun of the trackers hit and kill the child. The irony is complete;
the pearl which should have been the means of helping to fulfill
Kino's ambitions for his son actually has been an agent of disaster,
producing only suffering, despair, and finally death. Back it goes
into the sea, flung by Kino's hand.

The unfolding of incident presents Kino always as the angry,
frightened, but resolute man, determined to keep what he has
earned. This establishes the human element with satisfying dramatic emphasis while the allegorical element envelops the child
in a miasmic cloud of evil. A pattern of symbols draws the delicate
complexity of the parable into a tight design. The sea — Kino's environment — gives and takes away like a superbly indifferent minis-
ter of destiny. The pearl itself represents the wonder, the mystery,
the maddening, fateful beauty of the world, all in one luminous
sphere.

As well as in any other of his stories, major or minor, Steinbeck
matches manner to matter in *The Pearl*. The style has a subdued,
foreboding lyricism which communicates easily with a reader's
sympathies and never wavers toward elegiac excess. Because his
people are inarticulate Steinbeck must tell their story in the language of the heart and he is able to keep its idiom warm, believable,
and touching. This is perhaps the best of his achievements in the
role he liked best, that of fabulist.

Steinbeck, the analyst and critic of society, had in his time to re-
fute many charges of bias against democracy and "the American
way of life." Consideration of his work on this level of its interest

may well begin with a listing of the kinds of influence he did not aspire to exert. He was never a radical thinker, pamphleteer, agitator, Communist, or fellow traveler.

If evidence is needed that he entertained neither overt nor disguised sympathies with the Soviet system this may be readily found in his *Russian Journal*. The book is not one of his impressive accomplishments. It contains no striking insights and is content to offer merely a rambling account of casual encounters with bureaucrats, fellow writers, students, shopkeepers, official guides, Ukrainian farmers, stage performers, and mighty drinkers of vodka. The tone is relaxed to the point of being flaccid but what it conveys inescapably is a distaste for nearly everything that a repressive government does to its likable victims. Men are good, their institutions dangerous, he seems to be repeating again and again with a kind of unsurprised sorrow. In *The Grapes of Wrath* he had stated explicitly and by implication his dissatisfaction with the status quo in American society. But his comments on his experience in Russia leave no doubt that he had far greater hope for the regenerative power of democratic processes of government than for the arbitrary authority of any totalitarian system.

As one who believed in a writer's duty to try to keep humanity's morale high, Steinbeck believed also in the duty to expose attacks on its well-being. His two most searching examinations of the social scene, *The Grapes of Wrath* and *In Dubious Battle*, reveal clearly his ideas of what had gone wrong with the principles of democracy during the 1930's. He had seen men uprooted, degraded, and finally destroyed by the ruthlessly mechanistic operation of the economic system. He became deeply convinced that the rule of law and order is perverted into tyranny whenever democracy yields supinely to the demands of oligarchy. As propagandist he wished to do no more than to indicate how society, by encouraging morbid growths of special privilege for the rights of property over the rights of men, endangers its own survival. When it allows human beings to starve democracy squanders its greatest asset, creative energy.

Steinbeck had no precise scheme of reform to expound, no nostrum to offer. As an artist he could only observe and record the struggle of man against himself, hoping, by a vivid presentation of a problem in human affairs, to awaken minds to its crucial character. Without assuming the responsibilities of a reformer he wished to influence the temper of the time simply by urging acceptance of sane attitudes in matters of economic opportunity and attitudes favoring equality in the administration of justice.

His first book showed the direction his work was to take. *Cup of Gold* undertakes to demolish the inflated notions about the splendor of derring-do which have always tended to glorify the conqueror. This free treatment of the life story of the British pirate Sir Henry Morgan is offered as the epitome of all tales of ruthless enterprise. Out of the welter of its savage happenings rises the conviction that the most fearful of all false beatitudes might read: Blessed be the arriviste for he shall inherit the earth. What such anti-heroes really inherit, Steinbeck insists, are the rewards of all emotionally retarded creatures: memories of mindless cruelty and visions of a world pointlessly laid waste.

The imaginary Henry Morgan of the novel appears first as a stolid, determined boy of fifteen who leaves his home in Wales to go — as Steinbeck puts it with sly irony — "a-buccaneering" in the flamboyant style of the seventeenth century. He ships to sea, is sold into slavery in Barbados, becomes actual master of his languid, ineffectual owner, enriches himself at the latter's expense, becomes "Admiral" of a fleet of pirate vessels, and accepts commissions for bloody enterprise in international conflicts at sea. His crowning victory in Steinbeck's version of the story comes to him when he captures, sacks, and utterly destroys a rich city of Panama, the "Cup of Gold." With characteristic presence of mind and absence of morality, he manages to leave his followers marooned in the waste-land he has made and sails off with all the booty.

Below the surface of this ravening tale lies a pattern of symbols used to emphasize its meaning as parable. The wisdom of the ages is concentrated in the mind of Merlin, revived out of Arthurian romance to appear as young Henry Morgan's mentor. The symbol figure of Faust is reborn in Morgan himself. The grandiosity of his ambitions matches that of Goethe's heroic sinner though he becomes Faust's antithesis in his utter lack of concern for humanity. Echoes of Goethe's tone keep recurring. In the final scene Morgan on his deathbed is confronted, as was Faust, by the accusing shades of his wasted opportunities, his cruelties, and his crimes.

The clues to Steinbeck's basic intent in presenting so blasted an image of dehumanization are many. It is Merlin who anticipates the moral even before the tale has been told. Morgan, the seer says, will always catch his fireflies — that is, realize his wayward ambitions — if he keeps the heart of a child. What Steinbeck means to suggest is that savagery and blood letting — in general, heedless indifference to human rights — are the perverted pleasures of the immature. By implication he reaffirms the belief, expressed by Shaw in *Back to Methuselah*, that the race can save itself from its own destructive impulses only if it manages at last to grow up.

The man of aggressive, unapologetically acquisitive enterprise continued to be the target of Steinbeck's ironic temper throughout his career. In twentieth-century lore, and particularly on American soil, the buccaneer in the 1920's and 1930's often dwindled to the proportions of the excessively energetic businessman, the "go-getter" of the period's slang. Steinbeck never rested from the self-imposed task of shrinking this figure further still with his ridicule. The group of novels — *Cannery Row, The Wayward Bus,* and *Sweet Thursday* — which appear at first glance to be merely light entertainments actually have the purpose of challenging the values of a society that seeks to make a merit of one of its worst defects. A willingness to prey on others in the interest of self-aggrandizement is, in Steinbeck's code, the bleakest of sins.

The figures of *Cannery Row* and of its companion piece, *Sweet Thursday*, are idlers and drunkards, escapists from all the stern realities that control the lives of devotees of the gospel of success. The only rewards they want are those of the moment and their hedonistic activities as well as their buffoonish practical jokes conspicuously flout accepted ideas of proper behavior. But if they do no good, in the sense that dominates the thinking of conventional men and women, they do no harm either, which, Steinbeck says by implication, is more than can be said of many an enterprise of the righteous. The anti-heroes of *Cannery Row* are at least concerned with the happiness of one another. Like their brothers of *Tortilla Flat* they direct their "endeavors" toward the well-being of the group.

Steinbeck's jovial endorsement of this conduct is not to be taken as evidence of capriciousness. When he stands the accepted virtues and acknowledged vices on their heads — making conformity seem stuffily absurd if not altogether vicious and nonconformity somehow estimable in and of itself — he wishes to remind us that, after centuries of combining puritanical sanctimoniousness with Yankee cunning in our philosophy of getting on, we need to re-examine all our presuppositions about morality in the light of generosity and sanity.

Literary quality varies widely from scene to scene in each of these novels. *Cannery Row* contains anecdotes as amusing and as lethal as the best of his short stories offer; it indulges also in parodies of sentiment that seem more waggish than adroit. *Sweet Thursday* constantly threatens to collapse into a completely conventional boy-meets-girl romance, arbitrarily forced into a rowdy setting.

Best of the light entertainments is *The Wayward Bus*, which

34

Henry Seidel Canby likened to *The Canterbury Tales*. Here the reader follows the events of a journey and learns the life stories of the accidentally assembled men and women who make it. Under one kind of stress or another each reveals the animating impulse of his nature. A boy, called Pimples in callous recognition of his affliction, touchingly acknowledges his yearning for dignity and acceptance. A smug woman cannot restrain herself from opening the door on the untidy alcove of fantasy in which she lives. A petty man of affairs exposes the wasteland of his mean ambitions and feeble desires. A dying martinet compulsively uncovers the abject fear that has lurked in the background of his effort to be a tyrant. A prostitute testifies by her behavior to the fact that to be amoral in matters of sex is not necessarily to be lacking in sensibility or personal integrity.

It is not difficult to understand why Steinbeck chose sometimes to present in the form of raucous comedy his deeply felt protest against the false values of a property-minded, profit-obsessed world. The clown is permitted to make severe judgments which, had they been spoken in all earnestness by a declared reformer, would have brought the accusation of lese majesty down on his head. Steinbeck, when he championed the cause of the Okies in *The Grapes of Wrath*, had been subjected to just such vituperation. Though he was ever ready to fight for his opinions and his various literary presentations of them, it satisfied his ironic temper now and again to mask sympathies in ribald hilarity. What he is saying in *Cannery Row* quite clearly and unapologetically is that a society that permits, even encourages, high crimes against humanity and then makes a great show of niggling priggishness in the face of venial sin is a fatuous society.

It was appropriate that Steinbeck ended his career as he began it with a novel of social protest. *The Winter of Our Discontent* presents a crisis in the life of a man of sensibility, intelligence, and humor who undertakes willfully to live by the code of a modern buccaneer. The only reward that comes to him out of this adventure in open-eyed obliquity is a self-disgust so grim as to make him suicidal.

The novel is disarming in many ways. It introduces a new Steinbeck, entirely at home in a New England setting but even more critical of its mores than he had previously been of the blunted conscience of his native place. The central figure is a complex product of an old society and his sophisticated graces make him the complete antithesis of the typical pseudo-primitive of *Cannery Row*. The pervasive wit welling up out of the many soliloquies of the protagonist, instead of being of the locker-room variety characteristic of the lively farces, is mental and intricately involuted.

The intention of *The Winter of Our Discontent*, like that of *Cannery Row*, is to show how false the values of society may be. In the earlier book the theme of protest is treated lightheartedly, with an air of frivolous irresponsibility; in the later the tone becomes progressively more severe until in the end it seems almost grim.

Ethan Hawley, the central figure of Steinbeck's last novel, is out of sorts with his world in many ways. In part his discontent springs from the fact that though he bears a fine family name the society of which he is a member has provided him with no money to support the flimsy benefits of his prestige. His own ill-fortune has reduced him to the status of manager-clerk in a modest grocery store. His wife and children want more than they seem to be getting from their lives. He decides, on his family's account, to transform himself into a ruthless activist. The examples before him of a world that rewards cunning no matter how low its compromises with conscience may be seen to justify an attempt to enrich himself without concern for the suffering his manipulations may cause others.

Ethan's scheme is intricate and has several facets. With characteristic resourcefulness in the invention of incident, Steinbeck explores every aspect of the story's lurid interest. Crime and cruelty are involved, acts of shocking, degrading kinds. Ethan even betrays to his death a friend whom he professes to love. Steinbeck, one must believe, chose these instances not because he believed them to be sensationally extreme but rather because they seemed to him to be altogether too usual in the workaday world of enterprise. Loathing the mischief he has done, Ethan is almost persuaded to pay for it with his own life. The decision is reversed when he realizes that he still owes a duty to life. Only if he survives can his sensitive daughter be expected to do so.

Many symbolic presences reveal themselves intriguingly in the background of the novel. Its title suggests that Steinbeck was thinking of Shakespeare's Richard III who, like Ethan, is "subtle, false and treacherous," frivolously making evil his good. The dates of the book's events are significant. One cluster of events center around preparations for Easter. If Steinbeck's implication is that society is forever reenacting the drama of the Passion, Ethan is appropriately cast as its Judas. The rest of the happenings occur on the Fourth of July. Ethan's betrayal of his own principles is glaringly highlighted by memories of the day on which American democracy made its bold affirmation of the rights of man. The problem which Steinbeck faced in *The Winter of Our Discontent* was to make Ethan's tragedy seem somehow worthy to stand in the shadow of events so portentous. He did not wholly succeed. Likable though the novel is, it betrays — even as Ethan does — its own intent. The gravity of the situation is covered by a froth of frivolity. The tone of the storytelling is too light to bear the weight of its implications.

But the final comment on Steinbeck's work as critic of society must be that no other writer of our time has found so many ways of reminding us that man should be the beneficiary of his institutions, not their victim. His best work dramatizes the plight of man — now tragically, now humorously, with the aid of challenge, irony, homely eloquence, and subtle insight — as he indomitably struggles to make his environment a protective garment, not a haircloth shirt.

A curious view of Steinbeck, expressed by some of his early critics, presented him as a kind of naive natural genius who, having limited resources of technique and an even more severely limited vocabulary, blundered occasionally into displays of impressive, if brutal, power. Closer examination of his way with words should help to dispel that illusion. He was, in fact, a stylist of originality and grace. Just as he set up the structure of each of his best books in accordance with a well-planned architectural design, so he brought together the elements of his sentences with an artist's disciplined awareness of his own values. He expressed his attitudes, his sympathies, and his ideas in figurative language that remains fresh because his metaphors were entirely his own.

This was not true at the beginning. Steinbeck had his mentors. Some were good; it is not difficult to discern in *Cup of Gold* and *To a God Unknown* reverberations of the stately music of the King James version of the Bible. But the recommendation of others can have been only that they enjoyed, at the moment, wide popularity. One finds, again in *Cup of Gold*, imitations of the verbal tricks of James Branch Cabell and echoes of the self-conscious melodiousness of Donn Byrne. As he became more secure in awareness of his own identity, however, Steinbeck found his own voice.

It is in *The Grapes of Wrath* that the tone of the experienced artist declares itself with quiet confidence. The language of the narrative chapters is that of the people involved — simple, urgent in the expression of primal needs and desires, fresh and colorful within the limitations of the Joads's experience, powerful and poetic in implication. The chapters of comment presented temptations to a writer of Steinbeck's facility. Here and there a momentary lapse threatens the modesty of the style and the organ tones of omniscience swell out fortissimo. But for the most part these passages are kept in harmonic sympathy with the rest of the work. Steinbeck's lucid, generally unpretentious style enables him to present *The Grapes of Wrath* as a grave and respectful celebration of the dignity of man, a homely yet eloquent eulogy of the anonymous great who were his heroes.

Examples of his verbal skill reveal the secret of his method which was to make the simplest words and phrases flash into significance with seeming spontaneity. The quality of patience in one of his characters is established by use of the graphic simile "as enduring as a sea-washed stone." When he describes a woman as being "humorless as a chicken" one immediately sees the skitterings and hears the feeble, repetitive complaints of a creature ridiculously, yet pathetically, at war with a frustrating environment. The same genius for making pictures of mental attitudes reveals itself in the suggestion that the mind of another character — a Chinese shopkeeper who has forever to protect himself against the connivers of Cannery Row — "picked its way as delicately as a cat through cactus." One of Steinbeck's many eager digesters of experience defines himself unforgettably when he says, "I eat stories like grapes." As easily recognizable as an elderly female relative of one's own is the woman who has "a collection of small round convictions." The idiot in the story "Johnny Bear" has only one interest in life which is to cadge drinks at a bar; he keeps reiterating the sounds "Whiskey . . . Whis-key," as Steinbeck says, "like a bird call." By such small touches Steinbeck quickens his men and women into life.

He is equally successful with metaphor in creating landscape. Every season when the drenching rains came at last to his valley, the land, Steinbeck is inspired to say, "would shout with grass." A solitary visitor to a pool frequented by frogs remembers that "the air was full of their song and it was a kind of roaring silence." The modest poetry of surprise leaps out of such phrases as it does even more strikingly in descriptions of wild weather. An observer is warned of an approaching storm when he sees "a black cloud eating up the sky." In another such moment "a bristling, officious wind raked the valley." The device of making pictures of doleful situations is used to underscore tragedy: "Poverty sat cross-legged on the farm." Mood is established, the nature of a man defined, drama propelled by verbal devices so skillfully suited to their purpose as to be almost unnoticeable in themselves. Yet unobtrusive as these inspirations are they haunt the memory of the reader ever after.

The faults and limitations of Steinbeck's style have to do with matters of taste. Here, indeed, he did sometimes falter. It must be pointed out, however, that certain charges of grossness brought against books like *Cannery Row* would suggest themselves only to readers of parochial sensibility. The candor of the light entertainments belongs as surely to their themes as the bluntnesses of Rabelais, Sterne, and Swift belong to their satiric material. To have turned away in timidity from the obligatory scenes of grotesquerie would have amounted to artistic irresponsibility. Yet it is true that Steinbeck was capable of strewing a page or two with ribaldries that are conspicuously inappropriate to character and mood. *The Winter of Our Discontent* puts into the mouth of a cultivated man, Ethan, bits of verbal outrageousness that would have shocked the outspoken residents of Cannery Row.

The charge that Steinbeck's style is heavily laced with sentimentality should be examined closely on suspicion of bias. Some readers of *The Grapes of Wrath* brought it against him disingenuously, hoping to discredit his social attitudes by demeaning his way of expressing them. Disinterested analysts of his work were more perceptive even amid the near hysteria that greeted the book's appearance. Still, one must admit that he yielded to the temptation to be extravagant, at crucial moments, in presenting scenes of sentiment. Though he often used the word "gently" with ironic intent he used it far too often as he also overworked the even more lush "tenderly." And if sentimentality may be defined as the deliberate distortion of the probable in the interest of what is strikingly picturesque, then it is true that Steinbeck is sometimes sentimental, twisting his characters into dubious postures of nobility. The last scene of *The Grapes of Wrath* provides an example. In it a girl who has just lost her child at birth gives her breast, charged as it is with milk, to a man who has collapsed of starvation. Humanity, one understands, owes something to humanity which it must cross any gap to pay. But the symbolic act fails of its own excessive strain. It is patently a theatrical gesture used to bring down the curtain on an artificially composed tableau.

But, considering Steinbeck's temperament and the abundance of his imagination, it is remarkable that such excesses were few. His style contributed warm benefits of sympathy and spontaneity to each important book. Reappraising his work one is reminded that style is the man and that this was a remarkably whole and wholesome man.

A special dimension is evident in Steinbeck's work when it is compared with that of most of the writers of his time. He was not content to be merely an observer of mores and recorder of the movements of the moment. His books were all products of a speculative intelligence. The writing of fiction was for him a means of trying, for his own benefit and that of his readers, to identify the place of man in his world. His conception of that world included not merely the interests of economics and sociology but those of science and the realm of the spirit as well. Into the bloodstream of his work he released a steady flow of ideas to enrich its vigor.

An apprentice chemist in his youth and, in his middle years, part owner of a laboratory of marine biology, Steinbeck had always a semiprofessional interest in science. The scientific studies he engaged in, which were guided by a highly trained friend, Ed Ricketts, reinforced his belief in the oneness of all life — organic and inorganic, animal, vegetable, and aquatic. The book *Sea of Cortez*, written in collaboration with Ricketts, is in part a statement of that belief. It is also an account of a voyage up and down the Gulf of California to take specimens for a collection which, it was hoped, would constitute in itself a history of the marine life of the region.

What the investigators felt that they found in each tide pool they visited was "a world under a rock," a tiny microcosm of the universe. They comment: ". . . it is a strange thing that most of the feeling we call religious . . . is really the understanding and the attempt to say that man is . . . related inextricably to all reality, known and unknowable. This . . . profound feeling . . . made a Jesus, a St. Augustine, a St. Francis, a Roger Bacon, a Charles Darwin, and an Einstein. Each . . . reaffirmed . . . the knowledge that all things are one thing and that one thing is all things — plankton, a shimmering phosphorescence on the sea and the spinning planets and an expanding universe, all bound together by the elastic string of time."

Such passages have baffled some of Steinbeck's readers, leading them to the conclusion that his personal philosophy amounted to nothing but animalism, the denial that man has a spiritual nature. It is curious that his testimony should have been so misread. In his Nobel address he made two significant declarations: first, that he lived, as a writer, to "celebrate man's proven capacity for greatness of heart and spirit, courage, compassion and love"; second, that "a writer who does not believe in the perfectability of man" cannot claim to have a true vocation. These might be dismissed as the afterthoughts of an elderly convert, apologizing for the heresies of his youth, if Steinbeck had not anticipated such affirmations many years before in *Sea of Cortez*. There he made it clear that a sense of man's oneness with the universe should not drug the mind into passivity. Man is not merely the creature of an unknowable pattern of existence. He has made himself unique among animals by accepting responsibility for the good of others. Only he has this "drive outside of himself," that is, toward altruism. It is the "tragic miracle of consciousness" that has re-created him. "Potentially man is all things" and his impulses urge him often to be greedy and cruel. But he is also "capable of great love." His problem is to learn to accept his cosmic identity, by which Steinbeck means: to become aware of himself as an integral part of the whole design of existence. Tom Joad said it for him more succinctly in *The Grapes of Wrath*: "Well, maybe . . . a fella ain't got a soul of his own, but on'y a piece of a big one."

The theme of oneness is developed in *Sea of Cortez* with illustrations drawn from scientific observation. In an illuminating passage he describes the phenomenon of interdependence among aquatic creatures: "The schools swam, marshaled and patrolled. They turned as a unit and dived as a unit. . . . We cannot conceive of this intricacy until we are able to think of the school as an animal itself, reacting with all its cells to stimuli which perhaps might not influence one fish at all. And this larger animal, the school, seems to have a nature and drive and ends of its own . . . a school intelligence." His sense of unity stirred once more, Steinbeck pushes the speculation on: "And perhaps *this* unit of survival [the school of fishes] may key into the larger animal which is the life of all the sea, and this into the larger of the world."

This is the same concept which animated Steinbeck's imaginative re-creation in *The Red Pony* of the movement which he calls westering. As the old man who has been the "leader of the people" remembers: "It wasn't Indians that were important, nor adventures, nor even getting out here. It was a whole bunch of people made

43

into one big crawling beast . . . Every man wanted something for himself, but the big beast that was all of them wanted only westering. . . . We carried life out here and set it down the way those ants carry eggs. . . . The westering was as big as God, and the slow steps that made the movement piled up and piled up until the continent was crossed." So, as he might have said, the movement of westering keyed into the life of the continent and that into the life of the world.

It was the readiness to search behind the facts of life for a philosophical resolution of their complexity that gave depth and a rich texture to Steinbeck's picture of the life of his time. He had the rare ability to blend speculation into his fiction, making it an integral part of a narrative plan. Only a few of his contemporaries attempted to establish so broad a rapport with the minds of readers. Of such writers Thomas Mann offers the century's most brilliant example. As Joseph Wood Krutch once pointed out, Steinbeck's name must be linked with that of his European counterpart in any discussion of the novelist as thinker. Mann explored his magic mountain and Steinbeck his shimmering sea of contemplation but in doing so neither sacrificed the authority of his voice as storyteller.

Alexander Cowie has suggested, thinking of Steinbeck: "Perhaps this is the final responsibility of the novelist: he must be true to his time and yet save himself for Time."

Steinbeck was certainly true to his time in his eagerness to be identified with scientific enterprise and his willingness to take the guiding principles of science as his own. He might be called a moral ecologist, obsessively concerned with man's spiritual struggle to adjust himself to his environment. It is significant that this storyteller, conscious of a mission, undertook to popularize theories about the salvation of man's total environment long before public attention focused on the discipline of ecology.

He also nourished within himself the attitudes toward social reform that were growing slowly in the national consciousness of his time. His protests, his rejections as well as his affirmative convictions about the hope for regeneration, were exactly those that have been taken up by leaders of opinion in a later day enabling them, as teachers, theorists, and legislators, to change our minds in the direction of greater sensibility concerning human rights. Always the artist, never a practicing reformer, Steinbeck dramatized situations in American life and espoused beliefs about the need of room for growth in a way that helped to awaken the conscience of his fellow Americans.

Steinbeck was in addition a kind of working Freudian in the broad sense that he used the novel to remind readers that the myths of the past contain the wisdom of the race, that they tell us more about ourselves than sources of factual information can convey. Many, perhaps most, of the novelists of the 1930's and 1940's were deeply imbued with the same idea. But Steinbeck, consciously and conscientiously exploring the suggestions of Freud (and of Frazer whose work he may have known even better), covered a far broader field than did his fellow writers. His was an ambitious and inclusive effort to relate contemporary evidence about "the human condition" to that of the great witnesses of the past. His work suggests again and again that the story of humankind is a steadily continuing one, full of passions that seem as familiar in a setting of two thousand years ago as they do in our own time. It is a sense of the past made present that gives Steinbeck's best books their universality of tone. Old perils the like of which still surround us, old aspirations renewed as commitments by our restatement of them — these are the elements that contribute the essence of drama to his stories and give them distinction.

Steinbeck said that the one commandment of life is "to be and survive." His work may be said to fulfill that commandment.

↙ Selected Bibliography

Works of John Steinbeck

NOVELS

Cup of Gold. New York: Covici-Friede, 1929.
To a God Unknown. London: Heinemann, 1932.
Tortilla Flat. New York: Covici-Friede, 1935.
In Dubious Battle. New York: Covici-Friede, 1936.
The Red Pony. New York: Covici-Friede, 1937.
The Grapes of Wrath. New York: Viking Press, 1939.
Of Mice and Men. New York: Viking Press, 1940.
The Moon Is Down. New York: Viking Press, 1942.
Cannery Row. New York: Viking Press, 1945.
The Wayward Bus. New York: Viking Press, 1947.
The Pearl. New York: Viking Press, 1947.
East of Eden. New York: Viking Press, 1952.
Sweet Thursday. New York: Viking Press, 1954.
The Winter of Our Discontent. New York: Viking Press, 1961.

COLLECTIONS OF SHORT STORIES

The Pastures of Heaven. New York: Covici-Friede, 1932.
The Long Valley. New York: Viking Press, 1938.

PLAYS

Of Mice and Men (dramatic version with George Kaufman). New York: Viking Press, 1940.
The Moon Is Down (dramatic version). New York: Viking Press, 1942.
Burning Bright. New York: Viking Press, 1950. (A play in story form.)

NONFICTION

The Forgotten Village. New York: Viking Press, 1941.
Bombs Away. New York: Viking Press, 1942.
A Russian Journal. New York: Viking Press, 1948.
Sea of Cortez (in collaboration with Edward F. Ricketts). New York: Viking Press, 1951.

The Log from the Sea of Cortez. New York: Viking Press, 1951.
The Short Reign of Pippin IV. New York: Viking Press, 1957.
Once There Was a War. New York: Viking Press, 1958.
Travels with Charley. New York: Viking Press, 1962.
America and Americans. New York: Viking Press, 1966.
Journal of a Novel, The East of Eden Letters. New York: Viking Press, 1969.

CURRENT AMERICAN REPRINTS

Burning Bright. New York: Bantam. $.75.
Cannery Row. New York: Bantam. $.60. New York: Viking Press. $1.45.
Cup of Gold. New York: Bantam. $.75.
East of Eden. New York: Bantam. $1.25. New York: Viking Press. $2.95.
The Grapes of Wrath. New York: Bantam. $1.25. New York: Viking Press. $1.95.
In Dubious Battle. New York: Bantam. $.95. New York: Viking Press. $1.65.
The Moon Is Down. New York: Bantam. $.75.
Of Mice and Men. New York: Bantam. $.75. New York: Viking Press. $1.25.
Once There Was a War. New York: Bantam. $.75.
The Pastures of Heaven. New York: Viking Press. $1.45.
The Pearl. New York: Bantam. $.50.
The Red Pony. New York: Bantam. $.50.
The Short Reign of Pippin IV. New York: Bantam. $.75.
Sweet Thursday. New York: Bantam. $.95.
To a God Unknown. New York: Bantam. $.75.
Tortilla Flat. New York: Bantam. $.75.
Travels with Charley. New York: Bantam. $.95. New York: Viking Press. $1.65.
The Wayward Bus. New York: Bantam. $.75.
The Winter of Our Discontent. New York: Bantam. $.95.

Critical Studies

Allen, Walter. *Tradition and Dream.* London: John Dent and Son, Phoenix House, 1961.
Beach, Joseph Warren. *American Fiction, 1920–1940.* New York: Macmillan, 1941.
Cowie, Alexander. *The Rise of the American Novel.* New York: American Book, 1948.
French, Warren. *The Social Novel at the End of an Era.* Carbondale: Southern Illinois University Press, 1966.
Geismar, Maxwell. *Writers in Crisis.* Boston: Houghton Mifflin, 1942.
Hoffman, Frederick. *The Modern Novel in America.* Chicago: Regnery, 1951.
Kazin, Alfred. *On Native Grounds.* New York: Reynal and Hitchcock, 1942.
Lewis, R. W. B. *The Picaresque Saint.* Philadelphia: Lippincott, 1959.

Lisca, Peter. *The Wide World of John Steinbeck*. New Brunswick, N.J.: Rutgers University Press, 1958.

Tedlock, E. W., editor. *Steinbeck and His Critics*. Albuquerque: University of New Mexico Press, 1957.

Watt, Frank William. *John Steinbeck*. New York: Grove Press, 1962.

Wilson, Edmund. *The Boys in the Back Room: Notes on California Novelists*. San Francisco: Colt Press, 1941.